i love my love

Reyna Biddy

Andrews McMeel
PUBLISHING®

A Compilation of Spoken Word Poems
Written and Performed by Reyna Biddy

i love my love

Andrews McMeel Publishing
a division of Andrews McMeel Universal
1130 Walnut Street, Kansas City, Missouri 64106

www.andrewsmcmeel.com

17 18 19 20 21 RR2 10 9 8 7 6 5 4

ISBN: 978-1-4494-8676-1

Library of Congress Control Number: 2016959112

Editor: Patty Rice
Designer, Art Director: Holly Swayne
Production Editor: Erika Kuster
Production Manager: Cliff Koehler

ATTENTION: SCHOOLS AND BUSINESSES
Andrews McMeel books are available at quantity discounts with bulk purchase for educational, business, or sales promotional use. For information, please e-mail the Andrews McMeel Publishing Special Sales Department:
specialsales@amuniversal.com.

to whomever this makes and spreads love to..

i love my love

Reyna Biddy

for my mother's pain,
this is proof that sunshine comes after rain.
you are proof that beautiful things come from tragedy.
i'm so honored to be the result.

for my father's pain,
this is proof that real love stories do exist.
you are proof that beautiful bonds are created in silence.
i'm so honored to share my mother and y(ours).

for my mother
who gave me her heart,
we will never not be on the same beat.

for my father
who gave me his soul,
we will never not feel the same things.

for my parents' pain,
thank you.
for birthing me so brokenly beautiful.

preface: recollection

i haven't returned to this book since i left it. it's been an entire year. i've watched its growth from a distance but never had the courage to swallow my pride and revisit. each page, a reality i once knew. i've been too afraid to face myself. i haven't yet made peace with all of my truths. i anxiously gave birth to this song sometime in early December, without ever even knowing the meaning of "motherhood." foolishly, i planted seeds for a garden of healing, unaware of the process. i neglected the responsibility of watering then nurturing. as i watched the leaves fall and come again, i tried my best to sing. i tried my best to remember how the lullaby went. the one that taught you how to be a good friend.. the one that encouraged us all to love each other.. the one that forgot to mention how to love ourselves. the lullaby that never mentioned the aching. every day i'm in pain. i watched my mother die many times before i was old enough to understand what it meant to be broken from heartache. i was too afraid to ask her if her heart was still beating. i was too afraid to ask her if her heart wasn't beating. i was too afraid of the answer. i was too afraid of being alone.. so i always just left her alone. i watched my father take the form of an earthquake. my mother sung herself into an early deathbed. afraid of the reality of leaving, and what could have been or what could never be.. she stayed. i heard all of the nights she spent wailing every time she whispered "i love yous." and "i trust yous." i watched my father neglect those tears. i watched as he sat in broken silence. i watched as my mother held her Spanish tongue for the sake of an avoidable argument. i watched my mother give up on her happiness because the comfort of "till death do us part" was too sweet of a chorus.

the sweetest part in her song. i lost her somewhere along the lines of "how are you?" and "are you ever okay?" i've had to figure out how to deal with abandonment on my own. somehow i gave birth to the ideas that my father instilled within me. i began noticing as i made a habit out of lying beside bodies that meant nothing. he always warned me to save myself. inevitably, i became the villain. there became vines on my heart from the stillness. i kept trying to sing. i kept trying to put myself back into the place where innocence left me. my mother had died before i ever even had the chance to get to know her. the real her. every day i'm trying to find the parts of her within me. i was in the midst of practicing how to make love when i created something permanent. something bigger than i, myself, could ever be. i must have mimicked these habits from my parents. i've always wondered if foundation was ever even a consideration as the meaning to their true intentions. i was never taught how to love magic, so i could never bring myself to appreciate everything my heart had been creating. something worth reading when you're in need of saving. that was never even a consideration within my true intentions. i just wanted to write. i just wanted to sing my parents' love song.. more than anything, i just wanted to get rid of all the gloom and all the melancholy. i was sure i wanted to encourage people to heal themselves.. but i never thought it'd be through my story. i never knew how many people were on the same journey as me. one year later and finally, i'm ready to water my plants and my trees. i'm ready to plant an entire nursery. i'm ready to be less like my mother.

i'm ready to be more like me.

i'm ready to be more alive.

all in all.. i really just want to say thank you. to you. for giving me the strength to share my truths and for encouraging me to continue on. i'm encouraging you to continue on.

i'm forever and ever grateful.

Always Love,
Reyna Biddy

opening interlude

i've found a way to speak my heart's language.. every day. i've learned to
see the beauty in everyone and everything because someone once told me
a closed mind don't get fed and without soul food there is no growing, so..
i taught myself how to love the parts of you that even you are uncertain
about. this was written for you. i can only hope that throughout the
process of reading this, i will touch you in places none of your ex lovers
ever could have. i imagine that through my words you will pick up pieces
of yourself that you thought you could leave behind but your wounds are
what make you powerful. and your scars are what make you human. and
your stretch marks well.. they sing a great melody on how much you've
bent but love..

love would never let you fold.

i've mastered a way of giving the most secret parts of me publicly—yet
silently. so, here i am. writing to you—writing for you. hoping that now
you can see the beauty within the transparency in "brokenness" or the
importance in learning yourself, finding yourself, accepting yourself and
eventually.. loving yourself. i hope you feel the truths and experience the
growths and appreciate how invested my heart is—in not only my love but
love, in yours, too—and maybe you'll choose to ride with me down this
journey i'm taking to become a better me and my ambition to help you
realize that you're worthy.

Of Everything.

the beauty of being a writer and connecting with someone's soul is,
no matter where the relationship leads,
the love never dies when pen meets paper.

like me

my mother loves me more than anyone,
yet i can't seem to figure out how to love her back.
i can't love her the way i love others.
i could maybe be afraid.
or maybe i'm ashamed
to love someone *just like me.*
someone unafraid to bruise.
someone who knows how it feels to constantly lose the battle.
someone unafraid to be left empty.
i'm a lot like her..
and she's a lot like me.
my mother needs me more than anyone,
yet i can't seem to understand how to need her back.
i can't need her the way i need others.
i could maybe be naive
or maybe i'm too blind to see
what it looks like when
someone else's love for you is unconditional.
someone waiting to be loved,
someone *just like me.*

Loving yourself is the most fulfilling and beautiful love that life has to offer.
Unfortunately, we're all looking to love someone else..
we're all looking to be loved by someone else, first.

who i was in high school

you could call me your biggest enemy or you could call me the love of your life. but.. i promise there are no in-betweens. you could say i spoke too much or i shied away more than often. i never really wanted to be friends with the people whom i spilled my soul to.. and i never really showed the people most important to me the love that they deserved.. see i wasn't the kind of person you could love every day.

mirrors & epiphanies

- sometimes i love myself in you.
like teenagers on prom night,
i have no self-control.
i love me enough to hate this body.
i've run for hours in search of a cure,
shedding calories, ridding all the pesticides
that live inside of me.
it couldn't possibly be my fault.

- at 7 my mother told me i was big-boned
"like the rest of my father's side."

- at 14 my father said,
"maybe you shouldn't eat that last slice..
i mean, i don't want you to blow up overnight."

- at 17 i wore a size 13 jeans because
i had high blood–pressured thighs.
it wasn't until 20 that i looked in my mirror and realized

no one would ever love me for who i was on the inside.
not at this size.
not in this life.

results

the moment you said
"i don't love you anymore"—
i decided i don't love me anymore,
either.

pseudo

he trusts me enough to forgive my past..
and brings it up over morning coffee and midnight whiskey.
he loves me enough to look beyond my flaws..
but will never kiss me with love handles and morning breath.
he misses me enough to lie by my side..
even on nights he's home late, with soft scents of cheap wine and rose.
he needs me enough to call me on his free time..
to ask if i'd ever leave without a warning.
he wants me enough to make sure i'm all for him..
so he reminds me,
day out and day in,
that without him
i am nothing.

10 reasons i could never leave

1. I found you first. You were mine before anyone wanted you. You were mine before the growth and the grooming and I've made you into what you are.. you don't deserve to leave me.

2. Someone once told me to never make a home out of someone who doesn't love me but.. I am a refugee and at night I need saving, and in the morning I have four-months pregnant cravings, for a love that only we make, by the afternoon I get homesick.

3. We said silent vows as we stared in each other's eyes and struggled through the sand just to jump in the ocean so we could feel a wave so strong neither one of us had the strength to pull out of. You're stuck with me.

4. Remember that night when we were so drunk we poured our hearts into one another as if they were so full with lust that love began to tip over. You never really could sing but your lips created a symphony.. one of the best I've ever heard.. that night you said you were ready. Despite all my fears of full commitment, that night I made a birth mark out of you. I pressed you against my skin, delicately yet.. you became permanent. I remember you said you needed me.

5. You taught me things about life and me.. that I'm not sure I'll ever truly believe without you. Like how to love myself.. and how worthy I am. And how deep I can get before I ever let love inside of me. And how sometimes it's okay to collapse. Sometimes it's okay to relapse. Sometimes it's okay to miss everything you once were and sometimes it's okay to dip in the past.. but only if you're ready to be the beautiful tragedy. I'm ready to be the beautiful tragedy.

6. Some nights I bleed over you. I write our story until I get so tired that my wrist won't continue moving. I haven't reached the ending.

7. My body has a habit of waiting up for you.

8. We hold hands tighter than an infant holds his mother..

9. I've memorized the melody between your every heartbeat, just so I could sing it back if you ever get lonely. I.. learned the gaps between your fingers, just in case you ever need a hand.. I made sure mine fit perfectly.

10. **You promised we'd grow old together.**

halfway close

There are parts of me that
part of you wants to love.
I'll be patient.

rhetoric

How many times do you have to be hurt, humiliated,
thrown in the fire and burned,
embarrassed, neglected,
thrown in the ocean and forgotten,
lonely, bruised,
thrown under the bus and damaged,
broken, confused,
thrown in the mud after being used..
terrified, and stuck
till you realize that love doesn't?

love note:

i always swore love could never tear me apart until someone loved me better than i loved myself and then decided not to stay and took it all away. took me all away. then i was forced to deal with the pain. i was forced to deal with the bruises and stains on my heart. i had to learn the reality of loving myself unconditionally.. for better or worse. through the calamity and/or happy "me." i was forced to love all of me, entirely, regardless of all the reasons why someone else couldn't. regardless of every flaw that i allowed to have power over me. i was forced to really see who i am. and despite how much destruction any lover has caused me, i was never meant to give up on love. i was never meant to shut people out. i was never meant to save myself from hurting—i was only ever meant to grow from it. i was only ever meant to build and create within it. i was only ever meant to make love, to spread love, and to be love. i refuse to give up on me. i refuse to give up on everything and everyone meant for me. sometimes we break.. sometimes our hearts get torn into a million pieces.. but life is about building. and loving. and trusting that the sun will come out tomorrow.. or eventually. to the brokenhearted who still wear bright smiles on their faces. i see you. you and i are a lot of the same. always strong when "always" doesn't require us to be. trust me, you're perfect. you'll always be okay. be patient. happiness is coming soon.

i wander

some days i feel things too deep.
other days.. i wonder what it's like to feel anything at all. sometimes i can
feel the exact moment when everything in a relationship changes,
for the worst—it's like a super power.
that moment you look inside your lover's eyes and don't feel love
anymore. sometimes i can't understand why it all hurts so bad.. and other
times i can't understand why it doesn't hurt at all.

freestyles off chardonnay

one night i stared at myself in the mirror.
i asked, "who are you?"
i remember responding through my subconscious,
"i'm me.. the only person i know how to be.
i wouldn't consider myself gorgeous..
but some days i've learned how to be pretty.
my body's alright, but i could use a sit-up or.. fifty.
i wear hoodies during summer
because tight dresses are too risky.
more than often my hair is straightened..
when i was younger and it was curly
everyone would tell me i looked dirty.
i smile fairly big..
even when inside i'm really dying…
my reality sets in after dark
once i've questioned myself about why i've been lying.
i'm the type of person who's always running.
good things come to me if i'm lucky.
it makes me feel really good when he says he loves me..
but sometimes i cringe when he touches me.
i wonder why sometimes my mom barely hugged me
whenever she would—it was her tryna be funny.
i wanted to tell her about my new man from Kentucky,
but i know she knows he probably just wants to fuck me.

i guess i'm good at speaking because i have all these supporters
but what they don't know is i sleep in the fucking corner.
in a one-bedroom, living with five people.
'clustered like vintage finds from that one time,' words from a hoarder.
if they knew i barely loved myself, would they still love me?
i'm not really sure who i am.. or who i want to be.
i'm not really sure my reflection was meant to define me.
my dreams keep me trapped because society has confined me.
every day i get told i should model,
someone who looks like me shouldn't have a brain like mine.
but.. i promise i'm fine.
i'm just waiting on the day happiness truly finds me."
snapping back to reality—
All these things I never realized had me hurting.
All these things I couldn't let anyone say to me or about me.
It's easy to pick out flaws but what about the positivity?

that night i left who i was in that mirror.

- *I've been searching for my beauty, ever since.*

love note:

you're so much better and more beautiful than you give yourself credit for.
the word "beautiful" is too cheap a word to describe someone like you.
stop waiting on someone else to validate who you are.
you owe yourself some more recognition.

to all the boys i loved,

Forgive me for giving you
so much power over me.
You were never worthy.

my mother's interlude:

At 16 I was pregnant with what I thought would be a blessing
I never even questioned the commitment or consequences
Scared to say the least, but this love shit is all I got
To become a mom without one hurts, but I promised you'd have a lot
You were about 4 or 5 when your dad left us for that broad..
Took 'em six whole years to come around 'n' tell it all
You picked up the phone, member?
"Mom.. some lady Stella called"
One baby girl and a newborn boy that weren't mine
I always told that n*gga I wanted a big family, it just wasn't time
All we did was fight, he'd put his hands on me like every other night
I watched you watch me suffer
Then shortly after, as you was crying
You said "Mom.. Where was God?"
You kept going, even after I yelled stop
Trust me.. it won't happen again
He could get the fuck up out my house with his bitch ass lyin'
Fuck every kid he got and ima kill his baby mama, watch
Thank God we ain't committed by the law
He got me fucked up fucking around, but to go inside it raw
After everything we went thru, time hasn't made shit more simple
Hate to look my baby in the face and see him in you
No sight of pistols but he had me whipped around his bullshit
I'm sorry I fucked you up
Promise me you won't lose it..
Men have a habit of saying shit they don't mean then never prove it
Your grandpa loved to remind me that these n*ggas ain't shit
Wish he was a free man so he could see my downfall.

*the love note
my mother never
wrote me:*

Wow. You look beautiful today.
Every day you find a way to shine brighter than the last.
Every day you remind me that there's no use in regretting the past.
Every day I see myself in you and pray you have the strength to move
past whoever holds you back.
I'm sorry I was always afraid of lonely.
I'm sorry I was addicted to the way that men hold me..
I hope you understand that lust never lasts. And I hope you learn to tell
the difference between lust and romance.
There will be hundreds of men and most will do what it takes for you to
let them in. Most will love your bones till they ache and then they'll break
your heart in the end.
They'll sell you white lies and empty promises that you'll become more
attached to than them. The men will be sorry enough to touch where it
hurts and make sins with your skin.

Then they'll leave again.

Leaving you more vulnerable.. more dim. But I promise the world sees
you and admires how fragile your heart has always been. If I could be
around your whole life, during your loneliest nights, I would pick up your
chin. I would let you know how amazing you are from within. You know..
God has a funny way of putting the fiercest fire in our souls just to see the
breakdown during our emptiest alone. Just to see the breakthrough once
we love ourselves back to whole. Every night I pray for your well-being
before I pray for my own. I imagine you could use it. I imagine some days
you lose it. Life has a way of showing us ourselves through mini bruises.

But here's a reminder. You look beautiful tonight. Every night you've
found a way to shine brighter than the last. Your spirit speaks wonders and
your energy uplifts the mass. Wow. I'm sorry I forgot to teach you about
the light within that comes from
loving you before loving someone else.

message,

thinking everyone has the same heart as you
will leave you fucked up.

mellifluous

I was sure I swallowed your pride that evening
you moaned you love me as I was on my knees
wondering if God could forgive this too.

hostage

I wish it was easy for me to love you less.
I wish you were here to help me get through this.
I wish we could love like the teenagers who're fearless.
I wish you could see what you mean to me.
I wish I could be the person you run to, for everything.
You know I got you if you need anything.
You know my soul was crafted to match yours perfectly.
You know, lately I've been wondering..
about you wandering.
And why I was never enough to keep your heart still.
And why mine could never need you less.
And why mine could never want you less.
And why mine could never let you be.
And why yours forgot to set mine free.

3 a.m.

I stayed up late to write about you.
It was my only time of calm.
On my back the way you left me.
Silent yells of nostalgia.
You made us a promise.
Why choose now to neglect me?
My swollen eyes loved the bare you.
How dare you.

Why hurt someone whose only intention was to love you?

time tells

sooner or later
you'll get it.
you'll get me.
you'll understand why i kept trying.
why i kept dying to be held by you.

some days are much harder than others.
some days you wake up hoping not to be bothered.
some days you wish you would've never left the bed..
and some days you just wish the bad things could just leave your head.
today's that day for me.
i hope it gets better.

dear diary,

i'm starting to feel empty inside.. i don't have many friends these days. all the friends i did or do have never really were there for me, either way. i have a habit of going on autopilot and i wonder about the little pleasures in life that used to seem attainable. i imagine myself having "girls' night out" then crashing at my best friend's place because i'm too wasted to drive myself home. i dream about cooking five-course meals for my man and him genuinely liking every bit and piece of my hard effort, down to the sautéed asparagus seasoned with lemon. or sometimes i even hope that someone would hit me up spontaneously to take a trip to the beach right before sunset just to get stoned and share secrets we never could sober.
i don't know.. i guess i just haven't found my outlet.
and some days.. i feel i never will.
i look around and i see everyone.
but i don't think anyone sees me.
i fucking suck.
i suck at being social,
i suck at relationships..
i suck at life, overall.

i'm not worth it.

dalliance

I love you in ways words could never explain.
It's taken me time to accept that we don't love the same.
You mean to me what tulips mean to May.
I've looked you in the eyes to see the promise of a new day.
We're so fragile, yet so tamed.
Promise me you'll never consider me a mistake.
If I could go back to that first date, I'd probably say..
I'm not ready for love and all of its ways.
Some nights I stay awake and I pray
for a better understanding on why you've given us up
when you promised you'd stay.
You told me you'd fight for me.
Why don't you feel the same?
I lost myself trying to love you, what a shame.
To be in love with a man who leaves you astray.
And cares nothing about you or your day.
I've tried my best to stop crying, and..
I promise I'm trying.

I just want you so bad that it hurts—

easy come, easy go

You promised me the world then left mine black and white.
Can't help but remember who you were that night.
We talked about our dreams and our hopes for life.
And how nothing could go left when this felt so right,
like damn—

Shame on me for making a change I felt we'd both appreciate.
Shame on you for condoning my mistakes,
but now I'm the problem..
I fucked you up.
Huh?

I learned to love you the way you said
you'd love our unborn daughter.
So you dipped in it raw
while testing the waters.
And got caught up in your own lust.
But really.. I had plans for us.
You weren't sure I was the sea till my tide held tight
and you started drowning.
Guards should've warned you,
I got that good ting.
I've burned forests in your name,
I got that good weed.

Got me thinking,
about you, thinking about me and
why you left so easy.
Someone once told me
shit'll leave me
the same way it received me.
So. *Fuck it.*

love note:

it is better to heal alone than to fall under someone new.
you will only place yourself in a situation you are unready for.

lost & found

Lately I've been trying to remember who I am.

Or who I was.

Trying to retrace the steps I took to get to this numb place.

Trying to retract every man who led me here.

One by one I kept breaking.

Loving the idea of what love made me.

So happy, so alive.

Trying to understand where I went wrong

and how all of our feelings died.

I just wanted to be happy with you.

I just wanted to heal you.

I made the mistake of believing I could heal someone,

who's already broken..

and hurt myself.

Sometimes I just.. miss me.

- I should have loved you less.
- I should have loved **myself** more.

dear self,

I miss your smile.
You haven't been yourself in a while.
Remember who you were before society got ahold of you?
I wish you'd see all you're worth.
Every ounce of you is nothing less than worthwhile.
There're girls who'd kill to be you—
and believe it or not..
there're guys who'd kill to have you.
You fell in love and let it consume you.
Let love's downfall convince you that life..
really isn't all that great.
But babe, you're fucking amazing.
You deserve to be happier than
anyone else could ever make you.
You deserve to love yourself.
I miss you.
Come home.

love note:

you spend too much time guarding your heart and not enough time nurturing it. let love come inside and fill you. allow yourself to feel.. and if all fails, try again. be mindful that everything we do and everything that we go through is meant to help us grow, ultimately. throughout life we face many trials and tribulations.. we come face to face with adversity time and time again.. and we get hurt. hurt is a part of life the same way hurt is a part of growth. please, don't allow one person, or a couple of experiences, close you off to your own self-growth. you deserve to be the better version of yourself every single day. and by guarding your heart and shutting people out—you disable yourself. you put yourself in a position where you miss out on not only a love that's waiting for you—but life. you miss out on the most important things. you miss out on you. without opening your heart you can never truly know yourself. you can never fully love yourself. so keep going. keep learning. keep loving. keep being eager to learn and love new things/people.

to all the men i've loved

I GOT YOU
and not in the way your boys claim they do.
I have loyalty embedded across my lips,
your secrets are safe with me.
I have plans to nurture you the same way your mother did.
I picked you the same way I pick flowers—
I smell the beauty in them.
The thing about me is.. I was born to love.
I was born to treat you the way you've never been treated.
Ever wonder why you still think of me on your loneliest nights?
I mean..
I GOT YOU!
and not in the same way you promised you had me.
I have unconditional gripped around my thighs,

you could have made a home out of me.

I used to wonder why you've never settled down with anyone
then I realized I probably only picked you while in a rush.
I was so eager for love, so I settled for you.
The thing about me is..
I wasn't raised to give up.
So.. I really got you.
My spine was formed with elasticity
so I could handle both the downs and the ups.
I would have stuck around for longer than the lust..
but you saw no future in us,
you picked me the same way men pick attire—
you make sure to pick someone else before the season expires..

But I promise to God I wasn't lying when I said
I got you.

Someone once told me,
Real loss is only possible when you love someone or value something more than you
love and value your own self.

little me

my sister loves the men the way that i did.
hard, barebacked, with skin too soft to let go of.
her fingers are sore from tracing the mistakes his lips make.
she eats pineapples to prepare herself for love wars—
but nothing tastes better than loyalty.
nothing can replace her vulnerability,
she loves the men who are hurting.
i've watched her grow into everything they said i wouldn't be.
swollen spine and exhausted thighs,
every night the lies fill her mind with certainty.
my knees ache at the thought of
holding down the men who refuse to be held in the open.
my sister's heart shatters like a glass of wine when they leave..
the same way that mine did.
no one taught her that love was as permanent as footprints
in the sand or on hearts when the men abuse it.
i've watched her learn lessons no school was willing to teach..
i see a little me in her.
we became curious at the same age.
then we became experienced at the same pace.
my sister's body has maps that direct paths
to the points where roses blossom..
the same way that mine did.
the other women make conversation about her love
being a disease.
some days they'd say she fell too deep.
there were never thorns on the petals
but she bleeds from broken leaves and killer bees.
some nights the sky lights up
while the same ache fills her knees..

i always wondered what it'd be like to give away all of me..

but through my little sister,
i see.

love note:

love doesn't hurt. love heals.
anything or anyone that hurts you is not love.
people who don't know how to love, hurt.
anything or anyone that stunts your growth, is not love.
no matter how perfect it may seem—some days.
there's no such thing as a flower blooming beautifully—
without consistency..
without loyalty..
without attention..
without water..
without real love.
remember this.

enough

no more letting people in this way.
no more letting shit slide.
no more wondering.
no more late night cries.
no more trying to be the best me,
for people who don't really "see" me.
no more worrying.
no more lies.
no more lying to self.
no more being accepting of anyone or anything that hurts me.
no more hurting.
no more ignoring all the signs that are given.
no more thinking with my heart first.
no more broken hearts.
no more.

habits

Always knew you'd be the girl who loves too hard
after seeing you fall apart—
every time you watched your father leave.

dulce

I could treat you right if you let me.. I mean, I saw the way you looked
when you first met me. I know what it's like to be frightened by love,
but love.. I'm the type of love you've been waiting to see. I'm the type of
woman who can bring you to sing. We could dance under stars or drink
green tea in the spring. I could love you through the midnight hours and
put you straight to sleep. You see.. I'm the kind of person you've been
missing. I could love you so hard because I love me. I love me enough to
see right through you. I can see the fear in your eyes when you look at
a real woman.. a woman capable of any and everything.. a woman who
doesn't expect perfect and sees your potential.. a woman willing to work
with all that you are and kiss all of your scars away.. I could be the one..

if you let me.

hide & seek

i've been praying for someone like you to come find me.

crave me

if i were drunk right now,
i'd.. i'd say it.
of all the ways to express lust..
i chose to pray it.
i'm getting tired of these 3 a.m. cravings
and these sleepless nights where we stay in.
sometimes i wonder where you could take me.
same nights i feel i'm attracted to who you are potentially.
i've watched you grow into a person slightly suitable for me..
but i'm not really sure what it is i've been looking to see..
in anyone.
if i were high right now,
i'd probably say it.
your laugh's so fucking annoying,
but that smile.. i can't take it.
i can't remember what it's like to feel this vacant.
i've been waiting on your heart to come back from vacation.
how many times are you going to tell me you can't make it?
how many signs of pathetic till you give me some attention?
how many silent nights of lonely have I missed?
tired of being overbearing
but in the midst of stripping me without unfolding,
i can't help but miss your hands and how they mold me.
if you were mine right now.. i could say it..
you ever wonder why life takes love the same way it gave it?
easily friends, complicatedly lovers.
we made sense before you touched me and made me feel sure—
we were meant to be, you were meant for me, for sure.
as many seasons have passed,
leaving "us" in the past.

if you were sitting beside me and i was faded..
i could still get you fucked up on my love.
because some nights–

I know how much you crave it, too..

or however long

My alone could never feel as good as you do.
You stayed silent but your actions were fluent.
My heart beat fast like the first time in adolescence.
Our tongues whispered in harmonic eloquence.
Your eyes never wandered.
I was wondering if you could be my everything–
after I realized I would be anything for you.
I was wondering if you were into taking risks
and saying yes to challenges
because I want you to love me
like you've never been hurt before.
I mean, I could do anything for you.
I can still smell you on my skin.
Our nights feel like decades
while our hearts beg for centuries.

I'm sure,
I could spend lifetimes with you.

choices

I could hold you down or I can lift you up.
My love comes in many forms
if you're not looking for only one.
I can make your face shine like going south at sunset on the 101—
or if you're into rising
we can set an appointment to watch for fun.
I will massage coconut oil into your thighs,
spine and breasts—
or I can suck out wherever there is honey
as if the bees are at rest.

eloquence

Be good to me. *I dare you.*
What I would do for you,
might scare you.

Sé que no estamos enamorados pero dame un beso.
Let me taste who you were before I met you.
Let me figure out why they left you..
and if they left all the ashes
that remained from the incense
that were too intense to make love in—
I'm sure it was too hard to smell the fuck..
or each of the fucks that were given
and the lust that was in it.
I know how hard you can be.
I know how hard it may seem
to give yourself to a being
when within your heart lies uncertainty.
I know what it's like to feel empty.
You know it's alright to be open with me—
I've got no intentions of holding you down,
if you don't want that from me.
Tired of asking when you're free.

I always laugh at how bad I want you.
The way an addict wants his vice
Lovers want the night.
I want you in a grown-up way.
Not the kind of crush I had in 10th grade.
This is not the same.
Back then shit was fun
but this is not a game..
I want you to touch the parts of me

that other men are too afraid to see
and forget all the reasons you can't stay.
I know what you like,
I know what it's like to keep the best parts of me hidden,
aren't you exhausted?
I can make you feel alright.
You never really told me why you were into me.
I'm eager for you to hold me like it means anything.
Different from what you're used to.
Hope my persistence doesn't scare you..

It's just some nights I crave you
when I know I shouldn't.

trapped soul

why do you fight me with words
distant enough to injure my pride?
why do you feed me vacant responses
when you know how much i wonder?
you used to wonder what i was up to.
at one point i thought we could rely on each other.
you called me from New York just to remind me
that life without me,
wasn't as wonderful.
i wish i knew if there was someone else holding you.
i've always been good to you.
i know how much you loved me to visit you
when you were in town, too..
you gifted me your secrets.
you trusted me with your fears,
you even called me your "angel."
all the nights we laid together
making love through our energy..
you never did touch me.
your hands held insecurities
you decided to keep to yourself, but
i promised i'd never ruin you.
i would have stuck it through with you.
the long nights,
the pointless fights,
your tough skin that only i could get under.
i'm starting to see you everywhere—
and it hurts to know that you're no longer there..
or anywhere near me.

i wish you would just let me get through to you.
i wish you believed in all that I could bring you through..

i wish you believed in me enough to let me truly be here for you.
i just really wish..
you would let me..

love you.

message,

love is a beautiful thing, but without respect—it's an ugly habit.

my father's interlude:

Your mom's a crazy bitch
She was fucking on the low
While carrying you too
And she didn't think I'd know
Fuck everything she talkin' bout
Swear I can't stand that ho
It's just something about her love that I'm addicted to
I can't let her go
Five blessed babies, all from a different lady
I'm tied between the two, I got another one due—
Sometime in May or June, it's a girl
She'll be a Gemini like you..
Believe me when I say I didn't plan this shit this way
Jah's actions are mysterious
And I can't question my fate
For my life is in his hands
He guides the highways that I take
Every night I pray that all my loved ones look past
And can forgive all of my mistakes
I'm a good man, I never meant to hurt no one
Remember how I taught you
*Only coward n*ggas run?*
Stella 'n' yo mom don't see that
*I'm the realest n*gga they ever met*
Baby, believe that
I apologized for mine, so fuck it
If they leave me, I ain't trippen
Just take care of the fam for me
One love.

look daddy

My daddy always told me about how men ain't shit. So I ran around screaming.. "Men ain't shit!" He'd tell me stories about all the shit women should never have to deal with. One night he said, "Women were made with love and passion and desire and vulnerability and loyalty.. A woman has the power to make the strongest men weak and the most complacent man think. And men.. well men are born to get up and make the best out of their situation. Men have ambition and drive and respect.. the only thing a man fears is the day a woman will ask him to commit. And sometimes.. most times.. a woman can make a man feel so good that she turns him bad. That she loves him sick. A woman will love a man till he seeks a new love for a new high for a new drive to make the best out of his situation. And baby.. you gotta look out for you and your situation. You aren't just any woman." He was right. My daddy always pointed out who I could never be with. He always showed himself as Superman whenever my heart bent. He never let it break. He'd never let them take away the gold-plated trophy I happened to become when he realized I was designed to be the gem that he raised. He'd never let them make a tool out of me, not after all the talks about how delicate I was made and how rare I seemed. He'd walk me from home to the moon if it meant he could protect me along the way from men with resentment. You know.. the men who were raised to be hard, who fuck without heart, with the intentions of just a nut from the start.. who've lost every woman that made more than only love but spiritual art. With my daddy's security I never became that girl. Instead.. I became someone who was out to get the world. I was built to never fold. I was taught the most precious hearts were cold.

But what my father will never know is I became the men who prey on women who are whole. I became the men who ain't shit. I became the girl who men were scared to be with. My daddy always pointed out who I could never be with.. but Daddy? Did you ever fear that I'd become this? That I'd become worse than the men.. but a woman with a soul full of resentment?

I only tried to make the best out of my situation.

i forgot to tell you

i changed my mind about you.
i don't miss you like i used to.

bones

i used to wonder what it was like to be loved, for me.
i felt like if i were to lose all the acne,
someone could see me.
i thought that the prettier i could become
the more options i'd receive.
years later and i'm still just as lonely.
actually, i might be more alone than ever.
someone forgot to tell me that MAC's Ruby Woo lipstick
won't make it better.
that long hair, nice skin, and abs won't last forever.
that the men you let in are still out looking for treasure.
being physically gorgeous isn't a savior.
and having the most beautiful smile won't save him.
i forgot to hold on to who i was on the inside.
i wish it were easy for me to let people see what's on the inside.
i wish somebody would've told me
i was already perfect on the outside,
for the person who is perfect for me.
these bones have always been quite lovely.
these bones.. can't wait to be touched.
these bones can't wait to be loved.
to hold trust. to build and to bear life for nine months.
to be held through the roughs.. beyond the lust.
these bones could always keep up.
these bones have been bruised, broken, and cut.
these bones would never give up, on me.
or you.
i used to wonder what it would be like to be loved,
for me,
by you.

love note:

for anyone who cries themselves to sleep every night—for anyone who wakes up each morning wishing they hadn't—for anyone whose heart feels like an open wound. for anyone who thinks life would be better without 'em. for anyone bleeding misery from the inside out. for anyone who feels lonelier by the second. for anyone who questions their existence. for anyone who suffers hurricanes and tornados on the most beautiful days. i've been there. i get it. i remember praying to God out loud recently and i shocked myself when the words "some days i think i'm fine but most days my heart feels like it's drowning. today feels like death—only less people remembering to love me" came out. although i've never been suicidal i've dipped in and out of depression. i've wondered when the pain will go away. i've wondered if i was normal. or if this feeling was normal. being a writer.. this happens often for me. feeling like the world is on my back and i'm too exhausted to move. to try. to live. i'm fortunate to believe in the God in me that helps people every single day, but for anyone who feels hopeless and helpless.. there is hope. things will get better. don't cut yourself short by believing you have no purpose in this world. you're special. we all are. never stop searching for your happy place. and once you find it—keep it close. and please!!!
make homes out of something you can keep close forever—
not some "one" who's temporary.

endings

I don't want to be your sometimes.
I don't want to hear how I could have been.
I don't want to be the person who almost–
but wouldn't.. or didn't
because I'm too "temporary" to make permanent.
I don't want to be your some nights
or your next week when you have time.
I don't want to be faithfully yours
when you aren't truly mine.
I don't want to be your maybe.
I don't want to hear that you're
"too selective to settle down and date me."
I don't want to be an option.
I don't want to waste my time waiting.
I don't want to be your springtime.
I don't want you to bloom beautifully,
over me, so you can forget me.
I don't want to be on standby
until I'm who you feel I have potential to be.
I don't want to be the difference.
I don't want to be an example of
who grabbed your heart and who missed it.
I don't want this to be consistent.
I know that you're still out searching.
I don't want you to be the reason
that I stare out my window, hurting.
I don't want to be who you lie to.
I don't want to be your spur of the moment choice.
I don't want to be your more than likely–

if something or someone better comes up,
you'll let me know.
I don't want to be patient.
I don't want to be on your roster.
I don't want you to pick me
when everybody else is occupied—
or when everybody else has lost it.
I don't want to be your safe haven.
Don't come to me when you need saving—
because you would have left me in the sea of my own love, drowning.

If it were up to me we would have been but I've decided—

I don't want to be yours, anymore.

to anyone who wonders if they should
contact someone they "miss":

If a person is willing to live without you, then they should.

life is a lot more simple than we like to make it.
we run from those who love us and exhaust ourselves loving people who
don't. please—don't over exhaust yourself
by expressing your feelings over and over to someone who
just doesn't get it or care to. you'll end up empty.

10 reasons i could never stay

1. You weren't ready to dance when I was. You let my hand go in the essence of a mosh pit and I've been lost since.
2. The night you left I fell asleep on the floor of my shower. I was so broken I fell to my knees and asked God if he could take me.
3. You would have let him take me.
4. I was willing to give up part of me for you. I was willing to compromise my dreams for you. I was ready to be the person you needed. You never really needed me the way I needed you to.
5. I talked to my grandmother this morning and she asked me where the princess she remembered raising went. She asked me how I could be good for anyone if I wasn't good for me. She asked me if I was looking for kings who were looking for queens and how somewhere along the way I lost myself—so they all miss me.
6. You loved me the way my father always loved my mother and I no longer accept men with conditional traits.
7. As a woman I am obligated to continue loving. As a man you are eager to continue lusting. I was made gracefully with spiritual glitter and faithful glue. I was given wings that you tried to cut through. I was born with a voice that you tried to silence and a body that you tried to shame me of whenever spilling our love into someone else's. It took me a while to see that someone like you doesn't deserve a heart that only someone like myself was willing to offer.
8. I'm starting to find myself. And while picking up the pieces to my unfinished puzzle, I'm realizing that you weren't ever meant to fit in the picture.

9. You left scars on my skin that will never let me forget what love isn't.

10. You were wrong about me. You said I could never live without you. You thought I'd stick around for you to figure out how beautiful we could be but I planted scriptures in your palms that no one else will ever understand but all will see. Then they'll wonder what happened—then they'll ask about me. Tell them how I used to hold on because I loved you enough to never let you forget me. Then let them know that I've become forgiving and you've grown to resent me. I've grown from every verse I wrote and every word you spoke and you've learned my love made itself permanent on its own. You never were into practicing what you preach but I've decided it's okay that you let me go, too.

    I've already set you free.

i've been through a lot. i've seen and felt a whole lot. i've been broken and still, i've never considered folding. giving up was never an option for me. giving in was never an option for me. i refuse to sell myself short. i'm not afraid anymore. i'm not afraid to get my heart broken. i'm not afraid to take my chance on love and invest my heart into what feels right. i'm not afraid to just allow things to feel right. if anything, i'm afraid not to. i'm afraid of living a life that never plucks my heart's strings.

i'm afraid of dying loveless.

my dear,

It is okay to be in your natural state when
your heart is made of roots that birth daisies.
It is okay to be underweight when
your soul feeds oxygen through tubes of love-scented lilies.
It is okay to be a little late when
your intentions are to express lessons
by arriving right before the moon sets
and the day breaks.
There is no such thing as time.
Yet—timing is everything.
It's okay to wait for someone
who will touch you from the outside in
and create butterflies within your orchids.
There is no reason for rushing.
Everything happens the way it is supposed to,
whenever it's supposed to.
It's okay to talk all day about the kind of love
you've dreamed of before given the chance to bloom.
It's okay to be insecure.
It's common to be undernurtured.
Often, we overnourish others then end up in a drought.
But—you are a dozen roses and a field of hope.
You are every sweet kiss before they convinced you—
you aren't worth watering.

> *You are love. You've always been love.*

Weeds full of lust will keep sprouting
at the site of your growth..
but your season will never end.
Love, never end.
Because love never dies.
Your garden will continue to blossom
as soon as you appreciate each flaw
the way you do your strengths.
Then.. the thirst for something beautiful will expire.

You'll be alright.
You always have been.

love note:

women, by nature, are healers.
heal yourself queen so you can help heal the world.

beginnings

You played a big part in me moving on to me.
Sometimes I look at my reflection and still see you.
I remember you said you needed me like you needed to breathe—
but when you let me go I saw I was the only one suffocating.

I needed me, more.

presence

while you're busy chasing someone who doesn't care to be caught—
someone else is praying on your arrival.
someone else is waiting for your love.
stray away from what isn't,
show up for what is.

recover

sometimes your heart will hurt. sometimes your smile will ache. sometimes
your light will dim. sometimes your spirit will break. sometimes your
entire world will come crashing down with no warning, and no signs..
but no matter how destroyed you feel—you have to be willing to dig deep
inside of yourself to find some ambition to get you back right. you have
to look out for you. you have to let go. you have to place your focus
primarily on YOU. nothing about losing what's familiar feels good..
but uncomfortable places can be beautiful. growth is beautiful. you are
beautiful. you shouldn't have to wait around and pray for someone to
love you. you should love you. you should let go—because nothing worth
holding on to will ever destroy you. and holding on is destroying you.
trying to love someone into loving you—is destroying you. let go because
you have to get ahold of you. you have to retrace your steps and figure
out where you let YOU go. you have to take time to yourself to reflect on
when and where you lost yourself. you have to let go of what no longer
is—and accept what may have never been.. then you have to pick yourself
back up. you have to release any negativity clouding your mind and you
have to rid yourself of hopeful feelings. cleanse your soul. listen to your
intuition. learn yourself. let go of any bad habits you've picked up along
your journey and start over. no matter how bad or how much it hurts.. let
go and start with a clean slate because..

holding on is destroying you.

I wish someone would have told me that I'd be okay. I wish someone
would have held my hand and guided me toward the right way. I wish
someone would've helped me pick my head up and showed me what life
could be. I wish someone would have smirked at my first heartbreak and
instead of asking questions, let me be—then explained why it's okay to
cry—followed by all the reasons why sometimes life lets love die.
I wish I gave my time to men who knew how to kiss me on my forehead
and remind me that life is nothing short of beautiful. I wish more men
could see how my insides are beautiful. I wish I was taught to tell a man
from a boy. I wish my mother stood beside me as I looked for defects
in each mirror. I wish teachers would have encouraged me to follow my
dreams instead of study for SATs. I wish the school system told me that
my worth wasn't defined by my test scores. And I wish television showed
me that struggle is reality and I'd be happiest with emotional and mental
stability. I wish I broke less hearts. I wish my father wouldn't have cheated
on my mother and I wish it were easier to find a lover—nothing like him.
I wish it were all a little bit easier.. I wish I could speak to the younger me
and apologize for all the hurt and confusion I put me through.
But God.. look what I made of me.
I wish li'l me could see.
I can't keep from smiling.
Through every struggle I learned to find I'm far more powerful than
anything formed against me.
I just wish someone would have told me—

I'd be okay.

for me

It's a shame how hard you are on yourself.
You treat others with more love than you treat you.

You deserve to be celebrated, too.

me now)

for anyone who doesn't really know me.. i don't really make sense yet. i'm
not really in a place to stay the same yet. this is my body suit. these are my
creations. these are the words that i've formed. i'm a (godly) woman. not
meaning i'm religious, meaning there's a God inside of me. and every day
i talk to it. i'd say i do spiritual things. i have really bad habits, because i'm
human. i make excuses, because I'm human. there are no happy mediums
with me. i love hard. unconditionally. i still love the man who i rode the
elevator with this morning. i still love the men who've left me broken. i still
wish i could go back to that moment we fell for one another just to make
time more still. i still compromise. even when i know what i truly want,
just to make everyone else comfortable. it's been a minute since i've been
comfortable. for anyone who wonders what exactly i "do"? i do "me." i
know shit sounds mad corny but, for real. i make use of everything inside
of me. i treat my stories like they're symphonies.
and i been singing one hell of a song.
i write. i write my shit so truthful, you'd be surprised of what's left of
me. some days nothing. some days everything. some days i wake up
and all the hurt is still here. this morning i wasn't hurting. my happiness
came through for me. promised to stick around longer. promised to come
through for me. so happiness is what i've been leaning on these days. just
going through life and watching how this all plays out. this "forever after"
shit. this "happily" anything. cause that sounds like what's better for me.
I'm just a godlike woman–
trying to help people understand me better.

for you

You're worthy. Of any and every kind of love.
You were made so delicately and beautifully.
Stop diluting yourself to fit the standards of anyone who is unable to see
how fucking perfect you are.
It's not you, it's them.
Don't ever give anybody the power to define you,
alter who you are, or destroy you.
Your opinion about yourself is the only one that matters.
So fall in love.
As hard and as deep as possible—
with the only person who it makes sense to. **YOU.**

Q: What's the key to letting go?
A: Loving yourself.

Q: What's the key to loving yourself?
A: Spending more time with yourself, learning yourself, accepting yourself and how beautifully flawed you are.

Q: What keeps you confident?
A: Knowing I could NEVER be anyone else. I'm stuck with all of me. Why not embrace who I am?

Q: What can you tell someone who has major self-esteem/ self-confidence issues?
A: You know how long and hard God worked on you?

jeffrey

my mother has a new boyfriend. his name is Jeffrey.
i don't see her very often anymore..
so i can only really hope that she's happy.
i can only really hope that she's healthy.
i watched as she gave up on our family,
but i missed her leaving.
i waited by the phone for two weeks and never received anything.
not an "i'm so sorry this is happening" or an "i won't be returning."
not a sincere farewell..
and unfortunately, not a eulogy written within mourning.
i waited by the door for at least a knock. or a letter.
i waited to hear that she was at least "doing much better."
the truth is.. she found her feathers.
somewhere underneath the ash or amongst her new lover.
my mother tore down each wall of this house
the moment someone else made her feel the breeze.
the moment someone else made her feel at ease.
i watched as my father fell down on his knees,
praying that God brings him through.
for the first time my father's heart was broken.
there were cracks in his smile and silence in his speech.
my father was always my mother's water.
he refused to allow someone else to help her bloom.
he refused that someone else be the reason she breathe.
but there was no use in trying to make her stay.
she already took his power away.
someone already took his place.
he was only left to wonder when her heart went astray.
he was only left to wonder why her new lover
had to have the same name.

the little i've learned

Nothing ever really is all that bad.
You cannot make anyone love you—
especially when you do not love yourself.
No one will ever hurt you
worse than you hurt you.
We are our biggest enemies—
so we keep toxic people around
to devalue us consistently.
We pick up bad habits and give all our energy
to people who are unworthy.
We hurt ourselves the most.
We keep every door open welcoming the past
in hopes of closure from what has
already ripped us apart—
Our hearts are open wounds.
The more love we give
The more afraid we get—
but there will be more hurt in the future.
Our fears cannot protect us.
Our tears can connect us
from one broken spirit to another.
The universe can help us heal each other
but we cannot free one another's insecurities.
We break our own self down
and out of habit look to be saved somewhere else—

No one can save you from you.

love note:

lately, i've been extremely self-reflective. i've been extremely self conscious. i've been trying my best to not oversaturate myself with other people's traits or personalities and really just stick to me. really stick by myself so i can stay "me" as much as possible. i don't wanna reflect any of anyone who isn't me. i'm in a place where i want to constantly learn "me." i want to stop focusing so much of my time and attention on getting to know other people and i want to get to know myself better. i wanna learn the deeper things. like why i'm always afraid people will leave. or why it's so hard for me to open up to the people surrounding me but i'm capable of spilling my soul into thousands of beings who don't even know me. or why i always downplay myself by "sleeping" on me. i wanna understand why trust is something so foreign to me.. and why i always run when God hands me things.. like people. or when God hands me love. i wanna understand my love. i wanna understand my heart. i wanna know why i dismiss love when it's near but crave it when it's far. i wanna know why i've never liked to be touched. i wanna know what it feels like to be in more than lust. i wanna know what forever feels like. i wanna know why my mom and i are so distant. i wanna know why we're so the same but so different.. i wanna know why she left. i wanna know if i still reflect my father's ways.. and what it takes for me to stay on the harder days. i wanna know why i cry. all the time. i wanna know how to love me more. i wanna know—then love—who i am. so lately i've been writing this diary. for us both.
something to help us understand who we are better..
a diary to help you find you, faster.
a diary to show us how the same.. we truly are.

learning me

I'm goofy. I'm overpassionate. I'm clingy. I'm crazy.

I'll give you your freedom but in return I need reassurance.

Some days I'm insecure, other days I'm arrogant.

I speak my mind.. quite too often.

I bite my tongue.. quite too little.

I can make your world light up if you give me a chance..

I can make your heart soft and your head spin—

if we're talking romance.

I sit in the corner at social gatherings because I don't like to be bothered—

but the second I get you to myself,

I'll talk for hours.

Most times I'm too much to handle..

but **never** too much to love.

Took me some time to realize that.

future lover

my pancakes will probably never be half as good
as your grandmother's.
or my Thanksgiving pies,
my laundry, and back rubs..
my mother was 16 when she had me
so i wasn't raised to fill your bath with water.
i'm not the kind of woman you're used to.
my foreplay will probably never be as lame
as your previous lovers.
or my conversation, my dreams, and sense of humor.
i'll do whatever it takes to make you feel good.
i'll fill your mind with fantasies and fulfill your every need—
i know what it's like to love so hard i feel empty.
i know that i might leave stains on your nights,
once i leave—you may regret me.
i've gotten good at walking away.
i do not want the "where you beens?"
if you never cared for me to stay.
i do not want to hear "i love yous"
if you do not plan to show me.
i can smell fragments beneath
the *sweetness* of wordplay.
i do not want the "i miss yous"
if you allow our spirits to be distant.
and i do not want you in my head
if your heart is distracted
i will not play duck duck goose and chase after you
once i feel i've been chosen—
please be clear with your intentions.

i can give your fears the attention they need.

i want you to kiss me like we're 15

and our parents do not approve.

i can't wait until i get your best friend's approval.

it's taken me some time to accept the person that i'm becoming.

my mother used to remind me

to keep the worst parts of me hidden

so i made a habit out of hiding.

i wasn't sure which side of me could be considered beautiful..

i used to wonder how long God worked on me.

i used to ask God how long till someone falls for me.

he used to respond with thunderstorms

followed by clouds that were cotton-candied.

sunrises so genuine they filled my faith with certainty.

i want you to give yourself to me.

the first time we touch,

i'll probably smell like coconuts and serendipity.

my lies will probably never be as pointless as yours used to be..

or my stories about what used to be

or how i'm used to things.

sometimes, i find myself bragging about you.

over fig newtons and lavender tea.

the thought of you is quite calming.

unaware of who you are or

where we'll meet or

how we'll start—

i have something planned for you.

i imagine you've never dealt with a heart

like mine—

my love is unconditional.

i imagine you've never felt a spark

like the first time we decide to get high together.

my mind is anything but predictable.
i imagine you've never had to
squeeze your way into someone's schedule—
i've heard people say
you make time for whoever's irresistible.
my time is limited—
but i will never not wait up for you.

Every day I still wait for you.

every day i pray the moment we meet you'll be ready for me—
and i'll be ready to see the beauty in me, too.

new prayers

Dear Lord,

Thank you for the beauty you painted into my canvas.

Thank you for the morals you allowed
my mother to sew underneath my fabric.

Thank you for all of the men who came to love me..
yet caused havoc.

I am a better me.

Thank you for putting out my flames
every time I became fire..

Thank you for letting me soar to find myself
in the midst of haywire.

Thank you for sanity.

I promise there were demons on my shoulder that ran with me.

Thank you for allowing me to find myself.

Thank you for showing me the beauty in
growing out of things.

Outgrowing toxic feelings.

Grant me the strength to stay away from anyone hurting me.

Grant me the knowledge to know
who and what are wrong for me.

Help me to never stop choosing me.

Help me to never go back to what I used to be.

Help save me from the ones I love endlessly—
even after they've ruined me.

Help save me from love's calamity.

insides

i don't know what it's like to love me
but my ribcage sprouts daisies just in case we have babies.
lately, i've been saying *you're the one.*
i have aches in my bones that probably aren't worth touching.
but you make sure you fill the sections of me
that seem to have been abandoned sometime in early February.
i have sores on my lips from the truths i'll never tell
because i was once too ugly.
i'm used to speaking so deep—
my love becomes frightening.
i know i'm capable of scaring you away, too.
i don't want to scar you with all of my emotional abuse.
i promise, i will make a lover out of you.
i have the ocean amongst my thighs—
sometimes i forget how easy it is to sink.
so, keep on swimming.
keep on feeling.
keep on coming back into me with all that hope for infinity.
my right wrist has become rusty.
i don't usually write about people who voluntarily love me.
who unconditionally trust me not to fuck them up, too.
i can't promise you that you're right about me.
i have bruises on my chest from the parts of my heart i've tried to silence—
it beats louder.
lately, it beats harder. and harder. and harder.
i wish i could save you from me,
but you insisted on laying with me.
you found a vacancy.
so, i hope you plan to *watch the fires you placed in me.*

love note:

before we fall in love—let's heal each other.

promises

save me.. like you promised you would. like the promise of us after our
first conversation and how i just knew you could. save me.. like i still know
you can. sometimes i wonder where you go and if you ever need a hand.

sometimes i wonder if you see me drowning and if all along this was
your plan. and if you're waiting for me, patiently,
to say i can't breathe anymore.
between these mixed signals and temporary lines, i can't breathe anymore.
i'm waist-deep praying there's a way you can even see me anymore..
because i can't seem to see me without you, i can't continue to wonder if
you'll ever leave anymore..
save me.. cause i can't dream anymore. i can't fantasize about another
love like you ain't kiss my soul into a happy place. like you ain't brought
my life into better days. i can't give this up like we don't do more than
fuck like we don't really make love like our souls ain't just one like this is
something you can control like you ain't really in love like this was ever a
story about two fools in lust.
come on.. man.

if you can't remember the forevers you've placed in me..
look at me. look at the woman you've made me.
you can't abandon the home you've made in me.
look me in my eyes and promise me—you don't crave me.
let me know if i'm crazy.
i told myself i'd stop writing about people and then here you come. you
made me question if all the others were ever really worthy.. and how i
couldn't not write about the person who fits me completely and perfectly.

you fixed me completely and perfectly..

you know i love to see how much you love to see me loving
the way you love me.. it is all love right?
i know.. some days, you get afraid, right?
to have my heart, to be my rib.
to break some days, and go through shit.
it takes a warrior and a special kind of bravery to deal with
someone like me.
but i've decided i can't allow you to have cold feet. i swear i'll be patient
but i know you know you were made for me.

please, don't walk away from me.
not after you *promised* you would save me..

It takes a special kind of man—
to love a woman like me.

i told myself i wouldn't love again..
but you make sense

i admire you for all the reasons others cannot. the flaws you've let no one
see.. i, see, you king. i see the way you've treated me in the open without
hesitating. titles mean nothing because i'm a queen. yours, personally. we
talked about our walls and how guarded we should be but i've decided i'm
willing to allow you to damage me.. if it means i can spend the night, one
more time, to watch the moon play the strings. to them you're a musical
genius but no one sees the way your spirit sings for me. no one hears the
harmonies we make with love—without ever practicing. your heart is a
different kind of beautiful—you can't imagine the peace i've found within
you. your love has helped me pick up all my pieces.
i used to pray for a man like you but, today, i realize that i was too
unprepared—any moment before now.
i've fallen in love with you a million times in one night. our eyes stare in
harmony. we've never shared "i love yous" but don't be alarmed, my king,
i'm here for you..

whenever you need me..
whenever you don't—
if that means anything.

Still the same me—who loves *insanely*.

After All

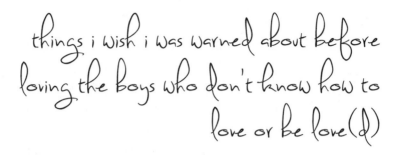

things i wish i was warned about before loving the boys who don't know how to love or be love(d)

1. Beautiful faces lead to ugly hearts.
2. He'll break your heart.
3. He'll look gorgeous doing it.. he'll probably look even more beautiful than the first time you laid eyes on him.
4. You'll welcome him back in with sore arms from long nights of holding your own self tight, tired lips from holding back the "I love yous" you never thought would come to an end and a bruised heart—only he could fix.
5. He won't fix you. He'll break more than just your heart this time— he'll drown your spirit—he'll drain your energy—he'll break your smile—and leave.. like you were nothing.
6. You'll lose him. And you'll end up without him for good this time. You'll be forced to pick up your pieces. You'll learn to love yourself. You'll find your joy. And eventually.. you'll find yourself.
7. Whenever, if ever, you run back into him—thank him for all the damage he allowed you to repair on your own. He helped make you a better, stronger, you.
8. He'll come back because he loves the way your smile looks before it's broken.
9. You'll laugh.. because he never was and never will be—worth it.

blooming

i remember i used to hate the idea of love. i grew up watching love done
wrong for so long that i started to believe it was a place or a thing or
a feeling that i didn't want any parts of. i watched love backfire in the
faces of all my loved ones.. i stopped believing in marriage or anything
permanent. when i was younger i remember i used to purposely get
involved with people just to hurt them. my method of protecting my
own heart was to not truly use it but to make people think that i did.
eventually.. i hurt me. i started to lose people and things that really meant
something to me. i started catching feelings for the ones who were no
good for me. i started falling in love with people who were just like me.
they'd hurt me, misuse and mistreat me. they'd show me the side of love
and myself that i was never used to. but i'm so thankful i saw her. i'm so
thankful i felt hurt. it wasn't until i truly fell apart that i realized how much
it took to rebuild back into who i was or.. who i was meant be. because
really i was never meant to be coldhearted.. i was never meant to break
hearts.. i was never meant to tear people apart. i'm a lover. and now, today,
i love that about me. i love that i understand now, how important it is that
i do whatever i can to protect and heal hearts.. by any means. i love that
people respect me and trust me enough to pour all their love into me.
i finally feel free.

ex lover

i remember i used to spend my time writing about you.
i used to lose sleep crying over you.
finally okay.
i'm happy that i suffered..
in both life and relationships
because i've learned, i grew, and i've evolved—
into the version of myself most necessary for survival.
i'm a work in progress
and i'm still working on a happier, wiser,
more loving and accepting ME—daily.
i'm still under construction.
whichever mistakes i make today—
i pray i learn and grow from,
but i'll never give up.
i'll always choose love.
and i know some days i stumble,
but i try my best.
for a long time after you left,
my dreams beat my reality.
i used to think about life and shit like
everything we could be
and everything that should be
and all the dead-end promises you gave that fooled me.
i used to pray that you'd find yourself
and someone who could love the baggage you carry on your back and i
prayed that i'd find some clarity and the strength to move forward,
without you.
i depended on your love for so long
that i didn't realize you became a part of me.

it was hard to see that
God placed you in my life for good reasoning.
i'm thankful to you for noticing me.
i'm thankful for our love and all the shit you taught me.
i'm thankful for our ending,
i was broken—indescribably.
i've faulted myself for loving too hard, for too long.
today i applaud myself.
in a generation where falling in love is conditional
and frowned upon,
i've spilled my soul.
i've let you see my naked, and sometimes ugly, truth.
this morning i finally saw my silver lining—
crazy how it used to be you.

love note:

any person willing to let you go isn't worth holding on to.

a message to women:

you deserve better than to be called "*pretty*."
you deserve better than to get upset and go online to act petty.
you deserve better than to be on "hold."
you deserve better than to hold on to someone
who's already let go.
you deserve better than to be held in convenience.

you deserve better than to keep your relationship "low-key" because..
"someone might see"
and
"someone might ask questions"
and someone might wonder why someone like you would rather hang
around a boy who won't commit when someone like them
is ready to love you.
is ready to learn you.

ready to show you—
who you are.
paint you a picture of you through his eyes and
convince you that you are indeed art.

show you the way he's mesmerized
by the way your broken heart still beats.
the way it flutters when whole eyes and yours meet.
the way it silences to express its beat.
show you how much he realizes you need healing from this hurting.
i know you.
i know something about what you've been through.

i know some days feel like heavy weights and hearts with protection that
you've failed to break through and i know what it's like to put heartbreak
on hold for the love of your life who forgot relationships take two.
i know he forgot to say "i love you, too."
i know he forgot to stay faithful.
i know you forgot about the time you promised yourself you'd do better
but every time you try to leave something keeps pulling you back–
telling you
this is the best you'll ever have in life.
so you stay the night. every night he misses you after remembering your
head and how good it works.
and how good it feels to know no matter how bad it gets–
you'll always come back.
i know you.
and he does, too.
we know the way your stomach drops at the thought of him loving
someone better.
so he knows you won't search for better
and i know you deserve better.
i know you deserve better than to have your spirit bruised.
i know you deserve someone who empowers you.
i know just how beautiful you could be if only you could see your own
value.
i know you.
you're a collection of paradoxes.
you're a compilation of food for thought.
you're a woman–before all things.
you're more a lover than a fighter–after all it seems..
you're special.
and i know you know you deserve better than to settle.

circumstances

If all else, if all fails,
we'll grow apart to fall together,

later.

what a relief.. to be a woman

To be a terrified, vulnerable, always-anxious, forever-worried, far-too-loving or far-too-lusting, loudmouthed, moment-grasping, baby-bearing, romance-obsessed, super-delicate, heartaching, weight-loss-eager, insecure, overpassionate, undercooperative, soul-throbbing, idol-worshipping, elegantly swearing, cuddle-needing, attention-seeking—yet always-grabbing, breathtaking, strong, and beautiful woman.
We aren't given enough credit.
In no way am I asking for recognition but I think it's important that women celebrate themselves. I think it's important that women continue to educate themselves, uplift themselves, speak for themselves, stand up for themselves, take care of themselves, touch themselves,
and forever and ever love themselves—
far more than anyone ever could. It's important that we remain ourselves, for ourselves, and stay true to everything and everyone that makes sense to ourselves. Sometimes we get lost in the idea that
we should be or look like others, but
all of our flaws are what make us so goddamn beautiful.
And.. sometimes I don't want to be pretty..
I wanna be fucking powerful.
I wanna be approached like a woman and not a piece of meat.
I want a man to look me in my eyes and say..

"What a relief.. a woman who loves herself."

reyna's interlude

I guess you can call this an "about me" or the puzzle piece that makes it all come together, perfectly. At 11 years old I told my parents I wanted to be an author "someday." All my life I was looking for a reason to say "someday," "someway," because I knew "today" was nearly impossible. Today I'm 21.. and I'm ready to give myself to you. I'm ready to share myself with whomever. I've learned that you cannot learn to love yourself overnight. You cannot rebuild your heart after being broken into a million pieces, overnight. You cannot fall in love overnight. You cannot fix yourself or your situation overnight. Everything takes time. It's taken me time to write this. It took me some time to see that I have a God-given talent and to see that my message is extraordinary. I cannot express how grateful I am to have been able to tap into the woman I was meant to be—who walked around spreading daylight on the darkest beings. I never knew what exactly I was doing until there were hundreds of messages in my inboxes of people thanking me. I started writing this book when I started questioning if there was anyone who could relate to me. I started spreading my truths and saw how so many people began to gravitate toward me. You might imagine how overwhelming that came to be. I started getting questions like "Who are you?" and "Thank you for uplifting me. How'd you learn to express yourself so honestly and so freely?" Well.. the difference between you and me is, I was taught how to love myself—but never how to love someone else. I was selfish. I tried my best to neglect my fears and love. Then—I tried to love. I've failed several times—but I've gotten up twice as many to where I'm no longer scared. I'm no longer afraid to learn myself. I'm no longer afraid to be hurt by people because I've seen the beauty that comes with breaking down to be built back up into who you're meant to be. I saw how hard my father loved my mother but it was never strong enough to be faithful. I watched my mom love my dad like he was her savior when in essence he was her Satan. I've learned

that the Devil is both gorgeous and deceiving. He's always had this crazy
habit where he loves me, he fucks me, then he leaves me. I've lost myself
in people I thought I was made for. I've lost myself in the person people
portrayed me to be. I was afraid of being me. I was afraid to feel. I was
afraid to bleed. But really.. I'm just like you. I've been in situations where
I would've rather died, too. I've been lied to. I cry, too. I've lost myself in
love so many times. I've reached a point in my life where I know how to
save myself from certain things. From certain beings. I know what it's like
to be damaged and humiliated by what I thought was love. And I know
what it's like to be too blind to see how toxic certain relationships were
for me. I know what it's like to feel like I was left stranded as soon as I fell
too deep. I know what it's like to pray for healing from the same person
who broke me. I know what it's like to lay next to someone and still feel
alone at night and by morning just as empty. I know what it's like to have
no one on my side. I know what it's like to keep everything inside. I know
what it's like to be too afraid to open up because of the fear of looking
weak. I know what it's like to be too afraid to give myself to someone
because of how many times I've placed my heart in the wrong person's
hands. I've given up on myself before. I've had ideas and dreams that I
never followed through with because I didn't believe that I could make
something out of me. I've learned to be more careful and selective with
my heart. I'm no longer afraid to love myself like I was taught from the
start. I'm no longer afraid of my truths. The truth is.. My name is Reyna..
And I'm an Addict. I don't know where I drifted or how I got here but
I'm addicted to love, not ordinarily. All my life I've been running from
affection in hopes of finding it. Instead of hiking up the right way, I went
down left.. thinking MAYBE prince charming tripped and needed some
assistance. All the while wishing there was no such thing because I wasn't
quite prepared for that engagement. You ever do something you know you
shouldn't then look for the reason why? Mine was curiosity. I've heard
plenty that curiosity kills the cat, but who molded the kitty? In my case, it
was my city. You see.. LA raised me. Taught me that nothing good comes

out of attachment, unless you like to feel pain.. Don't have too many partners, it'll ruin your name.. but needless to say—My name is Reyna, and regardless of the many obstacles, I've always remained the same me. And maybe that's my biggest downfall. Maybe I was meant to touch more, to love softer, to trust faster, to kiss longer, to smile brighter, to let the voices in my head win more often. Maybe I was born to question less, to live on my own, to speak a message so deep that the inner beauty inside of me slowly seeps into my eyes and you can't see that gorgeous little girl with the head full of curls anymore because that's not who I am. I'm a product of my environment and I'm addicted to love.. I'm addicted to struggle.. I'm addicted to spilling my soul and receiving nothing in return.. I'm addicted to being a better me and not every man can see the beauty in spoiled seeds but when that root starts growing, let that thang go.. and maybe I'll start to write something more worthy of anyone's time.

In the meantime, do us a favor,

remember to save some you for you.

Keep up with Reyna Biddy on social media
for news on her next book
and many other exclusives.

Twitter: @Dearyoufromwe
Instagram: @ReynaBiddy